Flowers

An Eclectic Collection and Collaboration of
Poetry Focused on
Growth, Nature, and Healing

Illustrations provided by: @jabeengadri on Instagram

ELITE PUBLISHING
HOUSE
YOUR LEGACY. YOUR BOOK.

Elite Publishing House
a Division of Blair Hayse,
International, LLC

2

ELITE PUBLISHING
HOUSE
YOUR LEGACY. YOUR BOOK.

First Edition

Copyright 2024 © Elite Publishing House
www.blairhayse.com
All Rights Reserved

No part of this book may be reproduced or transmitted in any form or by any means, electronic or mechanical, including photocopying, recording or by an information storage and retrieval system – except by a reviewer who may quote brief passages in a review to be printed in a magazine, newspaper or on the Web – without permission in writing from the publisher.

Cover Design by: Kathryn Denhof
Illustrations provided by: @jabeengadri on Instagram

Table of Contents

Introduction   pg. 6
By: Blair Hayse

Collection of Poetry   pg. 10
By: Mayuko Fukino

Collection of Poetry   pg. 29
By: Zachary Shiloh Watts

Collection of Poetry   pg. 43
By: Abby Weitkamp

Collection of Poetry   pg. 51
By: Blair Hayse

To those who feel all of the deepest feelings and continue to grow despite the pain, may you find a solace in the words within.

Introduction

Blair Hayse

This particular collaboration book was inspired by my desire to create a space where poets could put their poetry out into the world whether they had published their poetry before, was a closet poet, or maybe had never written a poem at all. I wanted to reach beyond the typical genre we represent most here at Elite Publishing House and allow for writers to enjoy the creative process that is behind another form of writing, poetry.

Poetry for me personally, has always been my vice when I was going through a lot emotionally or needed to put words down, but the emotions ran extremely deep. Those emotions could be almost any emotion and sometimes many emotions combined. However, after using my emotions to write, I always felt a release of the pent up emotions, as if I was setting them out into the world. Though, most of the time, they stayed tucked in my journal and close to my heart. I have often put them to music and sung them, put them in plays that have never seen the light of day, and in the notes on my phone to read when the tears fall. Poetry is personal. I think we all would agree, whether you are a reader of poetry or a writer of it (or both).

With each book I help compile, I am in awe of the authors and what they contribute. They never cease to amaze me. This book delivered that amazement with no doubts. From the words that danced across the pages to the emotions they each unearthed within me as I helped to edit the poems. These authors dug deep within and shared their innermost feelings and thoughts through each of their collections of poetry. Some tell a story and some express feelings, but all are beautifully written.

I want to take a moment to thank each of the contributing authors in this particular collaboration for trusting me with their poetry and to share it with you. This book would not be possible without each of you sharing your heartfelt collections. I also want to thank my own parents, who encouraged me at a young age to pursue my creativity and writing. Thank you to my children who encourage me to continue my creative ideas, no matter how crazy they may seem. Thank you to you, the reader, who without you...well, we would not be publishing this book. Your encouraged support is not only noted, but greatly appreciated.

Thank you to Kathryn Denhof, for taking my creative idea to the graphic design table to reveal a cover design that fit this book perfectly. Thank you to Abby, my editor on staff, who always spends countless hours perfecting each chapter so that you the reader gets the very best version of the book we can produce.

As you turn the pages over in this book, I hope you draw from the creative inspiration held within it. I hope you allow it to feed your creativity within. Maybe you too, will try to write that poem you have always wanted to write. Maybe you will share your lyrics that you penned to music. Whatever you do, I hope you feel it with passion and have fun. Creativity is not meant to be hidden. Share it with your family, friends, and even the world. You are a creative soul and that is something we should all be prouder of. Express your emotions.

If you are a follower of my books, you know by now that I believe in magic: the magic within us, and the magic that is shown to us each day. I hope you will find that same magic I have always strived to scatter within each book I publish is within this one, too. Flowers is yet another reminder that you are magic.

Keep the magic alive.

-Blair Hayse

9

Collection of Poetry

Mayuko Fukino

Symphony of Seasons

Blossoms grace the trees,
A tapestry of colors,
Spring's sweet melody.

Sun's warm embrace shines,
Nature blooms in vibrant hues,
Season of new life.

Crisp leaves falling down,
Colors paint the earth below,
Autumn's beauty found.

Snowflakes gently fall,
Blanketing the world in white,
Winter's silent call.

Red

Ruby lips so bold,
Scarlet sunsets paint the sky,
Passion's fiery hold.

Crimson leaves flutter,
Autumn's palette on display,
Nature's final blush.

Red roses in bloom,
Love's symbol, pure and true,
Petals soft as dreams.

Blood pumping, heart beats,
Life's vibrant pulse within me,
Red, the essence of life.

Yellow

Sunflower fields bloom,
Petals of yellow embrace,
Nature's golden hue.

Lemon zest brightens,
Tangy yellow bursts with zest,
Refreshes the soul.

Dandelions sway,
Yellow whispers in the breeze,
Wishes take flight.

Autumn leaves descend,
Yellow hues paint the landscape,
Nature's final dance.

Green

Emerald forests,
Nature's lush and vibrant cloak,
Green breathes life anew.

Dew-kissed blades of grass,
Whispering secrets of growth,
Green whispers of hope.

Envious envy,
Jealous of nature's palette,
Green with admiration.

Spring's emerald touch,
Leaves unfurl in verdant joy,
Green rebirths the earth.

Blue

Azure skies above,
Reflecting on tranquil seas,
Blue serenity.

Robin's eggshell hue,
Nestled in a leafy nook,
Blue innocence.

Cobalt waves crashing,
Roaring with untamed power,
Blue intensity.

Night's velvety cloak,
Studded with twinkling diamonds,
Blue midnight dreams.

Black

Darkness envelops,
Shadows dance with mystic grace,
Black secrets unfold.

Night's cloak, deep and vast,
Stars shine against ebony,
Black beauty revealed.

Ink stains on pages,
Words emerge from the abyss,
Black thoughts take flight.

Raven's wings take flight,
Silent guardian of night,
Black feathers shimmer.

White

Snowflakes gently fall,
Blanketing the world in white,
A winter wonder.

Pure and pristine hue,
White canvas, endless and bright,
Whispers of peace.

Clouds drift in the sky,
Cotton candy dreams of white,
Softness in the air.

Swan glides on the lake,
Graceful in its snowy plume,
Elegance in white.

Beauty Within

In stillness, we find,
The beauty of each moment,
Mindfulness unfolds.

Breathe in, breathe out, feel,
Awareness of the present,
Beauty surrounds us.

Like a lotus bloom,
Mindfulness opens our hearts,
Beauty from within.

A mindful gaze, see,
The world with new eyes, behold,
Beauty in all things.

Water

Gentle ripples flow,
Water's dance, serene and pure,
Nature's liquid grace.

Raindrops on petals,
Quenching thirst of flowers' souls,
Life's elixir falls.

Ocean's vast embrace,
Majestic waves, ebb and flow,
Endless mystery.

Crystal streams meander,
Nature's melody unfolds,
Water's soothing song.

Fire

Flames dance and flicker,
Burning bright with fierce passion,
Fire's wild embrace.

Warmth on a cold night,
Crackling logs in the hearth glow,
Fire's comforting touch.

Sparks leap to the sky,
Burning embers float away,
Fire's ephemeral flight.

Fire's destructive force,
Power untamed and untamed,
Beware its fiery wrath.

Baku

Baku flies at night,
Guardian of dreams and sleep,
Whisking nightmares away.

Wings of ebony,
Baku soars through starlit sky,
Protecting all dreams.

Celestial beast,
Baku roams the heavens high,
Bringing peace and rest.

Night's mythical friend,
Baku, the dream-eating bat,
In the sky, his realm extends.

Sun

Golden rays cascade,
A fiery ball in the sky,
Sun's warmth on my face.

Morning sun rises,
Painting the world with colors,
Nature awakens.

Sun sets in the west,
A brilliant farewell show,
Day gives way to night.

Sun's gentle caress,
Nurturing life with its light,
A beacon of hope.

Moon

Crescent moon shines bright,
Silver glow in the night sky,
Whispers of dreams.

Full moon's gentle grace,
Illuminating the dark,
Guiding lost souls.

Moonlight dances on,
Casting shadows on the Earth,
Mysteries unfold.

 Moon's tranquil presence,
A muse for poets and hearts,
Inspiring love.

Stars

Twinkling stars above,
Guiding us through the darkness,
Hope in their embrace.

Shooting star so bright,
Grant my wish upon your flight,
Fleeting beauty's light.

Countless stars align,
A cosmic tapestry shines,
Universe's sign.

Stars in the night sky,
Ignite dreams with their pure light,
Endless possibilities.

Gaia

Gaia, Mother Earth,
Nurturing all life with love,
Her divine beauty.

Seasons come and go,
Gaia's ever-changing dance,
Nature's symphony.

Mountains touch the sky,
Rivers flowing through her veins,
Gaia's majesty.

Forests lush and green,
Gaia's lungs, breathing life in,
Sacred and serene.

About Mayuko Fukino:

Mayuko is a mindful life coach, yoga teacher, ancient wisdom keeper, and Japanese language teacher. Recently having completed her Bachelor's degree in Psychology, she seamlessly integrates evidence-based psychological knowledge into her holistic approach to life coaching, marrying science with spirituality and mind with body practice.

With a deep connection to nature, she finds solace in the serenade of the sky and cherishes the harmonious melodies sung by all beings on Earth. Her journey towards self-discovery and inner peace, now enriched by her psychological training, has led her to embrace ancient wisdom and share its teachings with others.

As a coach, she guides individuals on a path of mindfulness, incorporating evidence-based practices to help them cultivate self-awareness and find balance in their lives. Combining movement and breath, she creates a sacred space in her yoga classes for students to explore their bodies and minds, infusing them with both psychological insights and ancient wisdom.

In addition to teaching the Japanese language, Mayuko imparts the wisdom of Japanese ancient traditions, inviting students to delve into the rich cultural heritage and profound wisdom of Japan. With a compassionate heart and gentle spirit, she is dedicated to supporting others on their journey towards a mindful and fulfilling life, seamlessly integrating psychological knowledge, ancient wisdom, and the practices of the mind and body.

You can connect with Mayuko here:

Facebook: https://www.facebook.com/MayukoTLC365

Instagram: https://www.instagram.com/mindfulmayuko/

Collection of Poetry

Zachary Shiloh Watts

Transition

It's a time of change
Gets one out of their comfortable range
It's saying goodbye
When a person or relationship dies
It's looking up at the sky
Hearing the answer to a question of why
To build an individual's clout
It's going through all kinds of doubt
For some, it takes years to find
Brings about clarity of mind
Living life with pure vision
These are my definitions of transition

Spring

This is my favorite season
There are different reasons
The weather isn't quite cold
Nature becomes more bold
Time stops going slow
Life has a stronger flow
It's time for big dreams
Hanging out by public scenes
Setting aside ifs, buts, and maybes
Welcoming the birth of babies
Turning frowns to smiles
Not just for a little while
These blessed things
Manifest strongly in Spring

Silence

It is starting the day with no sound
It is being one with the ground
It is a daily reminder to me
I am still like a tree
There is no guilt or shame
There is no one to play a game
Time to clean a mess
Allow the reduction of stress
No holding onto a fence
I appreciate my silence

In the Midst of CHAOS

It is something I know well
How to survive a living Hell
What it is to have lack of money
With and without a human honey
How to live in light
Especially when things don't go right
Not wanting to be in your head
Days to stay in bed
To pivot a noble plan
After being in unhealthy hands
To be the real you
Even if your attitude comes off rude
To let go of more than one cross
This is living 'In The Midst of CHAOS'

God

Known by numerous labels
Some would call this a fable
Many believe this is a man in the sky
I say my greatest reason why I'm alive
Love and saving grace
Without a human face
Communicates with a small, calm voice
Reminds me I have more than one choice
Presence I can't dismiss
Provider of eternal bliss
Can be odd
This, for me, best defines the almighty God

Poetry

Written with emotion
I believe that notion
Made on colorful pages
Created at different ages
Words used are real
Help convey what one feels
Doesn't ask adults to pay tax
Comes together when one does relax
Has no sense of time
Doesn't have to necessarily rhyme
There is no need to fight
No "Who is wrong or right"
Lines can be small
Sentences can be tall
Some are set to a beat
Others are read on feet
The biggest goal
Is to connect numerous souls
Paid or free
This motion is called poetry

Nobody Can Be You

Sit down over here
Lend me an ear
You are not weak
You have overcome your share of peaks
Whether or not you have been to college
You possess unique knowledge
Being like someone else
Doesn't completely create wealth
There is no need to hide
What you have deep inside
Step away from your place of birth
Share yourself with the Earth
Whenever sad or blue
One thing is absolutely true
Remember that nobody can be you

Fun

It is hanging out with friends
Regardless of weekdays or weekends
It is getting your hook
Into reading or writing a book
It is relieving stress
After failing or passing a test
Not always being in a seat
Simple as moving your feet
It is banging a drum
As you hear someone hum
It is making silly faces
With people of all races
Being in a trance
As you watch folks dance
When all is said and done
That's having fun

Help

It is giving advice
When someone is not alright
It is following the signs
From the divine
It is as simple as a prayer
To show how much you care
It is accepting a donation
For community restoration
It is someone fully believing
In what you are achieving
It is not going "Oh welp"
All the above is how to help

Gratitude

It is having an open heart
After being torn apart
It is a feeling
That provides healing
A genuine practice every day
Once applied, you'll never stray
It is an appreciation for what you got
Will manifest opportunities white hot
Expression comes in dance
I believe it is a factor in growing romance
Woman or dude
It is available to you
This is my truth
I end with gratitude

About Zachary Shiloh Watts:

Zachary Shiloh Watts is an all-life New Yorker. He was born in Brooklyn, NY (during the winter of 1987). Has resided in Staten Island (since 1997). He is the proud middle of three children.

His favorite season is Spring. His favorite color is red. When talking with Zach, he tends to not cuss. Should he curse then it goes with what he is conveying (at the time). He loves being in nature. Weight trains 3X (or more) a week.

When he isn't working, Zach is pursuing his wildest dreams. One of them happens to be his love of writing. He has the honor of saying he is a Best-Selling Author. His next book release is his second memoir called In The Midst of CHAOS: MANIFESTING Life With The Infinite.

Another passion is the expansion of what he calls BLK Lion's Airspace. What is BLK? BLK is short for black.

BLK Lion's Airspace is The Flowtastic Zone where LOVE shines brightest. Home of the BLK Lion's Domain interview segment (where Universal Grounding is partaken). He discusses Universal Laws (more so Law of Attraction), writing, health and whatever else keeps him highly vibrational. His podcast has been around since June 16, 2019.

The most important thing to Zachary Shiloh is his online coaching business. It was known as Love's Roar from 2020. One half of what was called Fear to Love's Roar in Summer 2021. Since April 28, 2022, it roars as Mind Over Matter Unlimited.

Mind Over Matter Unlimited isn't your typical weight loss. It is where health resurrection MANIFESTS. It STARTS in the MIND. What FOLLOWS will AWE you.

Please contact and support Zachary Shiloh by using the provided links:

https://www.facebook.com/BLKLion130/

https://twitter.com/BLKLion130

https://www.instagram.com/blklion130/

Zacharys.watts@yahoo.com

Zacshi130@gmail.com

42

Collection of Poetry

Abby Weitkamp

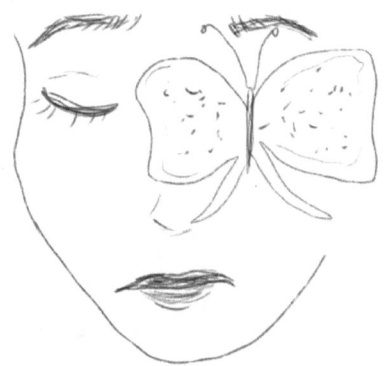

Chrysanthemum

Chrysanthemum's the word
When you mistreat me.
Yellow I am
While you Cheshire grin.
What is that smell?
Decay from the inside out,
Yet no one is poisoned
From feasting
On your flesh

Except me.

"Shhh."

Tulips

Two lips
Pushed together in rage.
Strangled in the throat
Is the voice
That cries out
In silence.
Powerless
To be powerful
Is the neglected seed
Left to die.
All rain,
No sun.
Two lips
Pushed apart in agony.

46

Not

Born to be
Protected by him,
Wired to see
His role modeled.
He loves me.

Forced to be
Violated by him,
Taught to think
It was special.
He loves me not.

Fated to make
His acquaintance one day,
Hugged into trusting
This was safe.
He loves me.

Drugged to meet
His lustful demands,
Left all alone
To plot my end.
He loves me
Not.

Dissonance

"Hello, me,
How are you today?"

"I am fine
Unless you try that shit again."

"What do you mean?
Don't you want to get better?
Don't you want to be happy?
Don't you want to feel fulfilled?"

"No.

I just want to be safe."

Enemy

In the mirror
I see you,
With your auburn hair
And your eyes dull blue,
With your mind exacting,
Your answers planned out,
Your cutting words
And raging self-doubt,
Your careful ways
And your mood so low,
With the negative truths
You think you know.
The more I stare,
The more I see.
In the mirror
There is you,
Staring right back at me.

About Abby Weitkamp:

Abby is an Assistant and Editor Intern at Elite Publishing House and Girl on Fire Magazine. She is also a mom who just recently picked up her pen and paper, dusted off the cobwebs, and committed to being creative again. As a kid, she wrote short stories and poetry all the time and she thinks it is high time she gets back to it. Most of her time is spent chasing a toddler around, but you can also find her cackling with her husband, tending to animals both inside and outside her home, listening to music, spending time in nature, and eating the best food her dietary restrictions will allow.

You can find Abby on social media here:

https://www.facebook.com/abagayle.copp

https://www.instagram.com/abbyweitkamp/

Collection of Poetry

Blair Hayse

How it Would End...

It's been a very long time
Since I missed you the way I have today.
I missed your sweet smile
And the laughter you always made.

I miss how you made me laugh
Until I couldn't breathe anymore.
When my world was upside down
You always righted the wrong.

You certainly weren't perfect,
But neither was I.
Sometimes life seems so miserable
With you gone and not by my side.

I tell myself to be strong
And that you would tell me the same,
But you were the strong one
Who always carried me.

When life fell in pieces
You made it perfect again
And I always could trust you.
You were my very best friend.

I ran across a letter
You wrote me long ago.
Told me I was your angel
And that I was sent from heaven above.

I ran across our photos
And the memories that we shared.
I sat there and cried
Until I had nothing left.

Life seems so blank
Without you by my side.
It wasn't supposed to end this way.
We had plans for a long, long life.

Plans to grow old together
And travel the world wide.
I wasn't supposed to face this all alone.
You were supposed to be here;
To heal my broken heart.

I wasn't supposed to have to tell my kids
Stories of a dad they never knew.
You were supposed to be here
So, they could live those memories with you.

I wasn't supposed to wish
That I could freeze the time.
In hopes of catching memories with the kids
To let you see it through my eyes.

I wasn't supposed to think
That time would heal the pain.

54

That life would get easier
The longer you were away.

I still miss you
With every passing day.
Just when I think I can be happy again;
I'm flooded with pain.

Pain of memories gone
And love that was too short.
A marriage made of two lovers
Who fought a lot of storms.

You taught me so much
In those years we had.
I hope you know
You are in my heart,
Till the end.

No other happiness
Can replace what has been.
If given a choice to do it all again,
I would pick our life
Even though I now know
How it would end.

Rain, Rain...

Rain, Rain...

Rain drops don't go away

They fall down just to stay.

I keep waiting on the sun

Just a peek of it I would love.

But somewhere

In this stormy sky

I see lighting crashing to the ground.

I hear thunder clapping loudly all around

As if it's happy to see me standing there

With no umbrella and wet hair.

Guess if it's gonna rain this hard

I'll learn to dance away the storm.

Rain, rain

Don't go away

I'm here to play.

Rain, rain

Please do stay

Take me by the hand, lead this dance.

Rain, rain

Keep pouring down

Some of us find solace there.

Rain, rain

Say my name, make me strong

Drown out the pain.

They say lighting don't strike

The same place twice

So, I'm safe to stand my ground,

I've already had it hit me down.

Some people see more rain than sun,

My life story — the rain I've come to love.

My fear of most storms

Has been erased with comfort in its place.

I guess when rain starts to pour

There is no need to fear or run,

Stand there — soak it in

Feel it sink into your skin.

Rain, rain

Warm me with your embrace

Kiss me with reminders of the pain.

Rain, rain

Come take me home

Flood my soul with your cold.

Rain, rain

You made me strong

Because of you I dance my song.

58

Rain, rain

Still my heart

Keep pouring down

Some of us find solace there.

Umbrella

Umbrella
Where are you?

You catch the rain
But can you catch the tears too?

I can barely see,
Is the haze from the rain?

I keep on blinking,
Why is the rain not leaving?

The tears keep falling
Like rain on a dry, dry earth

But I keep looking
For the umbrella that can save me
From the water above.

Do you feel the rain?
Do you feel the tears?
Are you left confused?

Where is the umbrella
That offers me protection?

60

Can it be found?
Or was that just a myth?
The truth is
There is no umbrella to be found.

The rain must come,
The tears must fall,
And those who weather the storm
Will be promised to be strong.

But what if I do not want strong?
What if I do not want to weather the rain?
Is there a ticket back to where I came?

Umbrella,
You are a lie.

I will keep on moving forward
Even when I want to die.

Somehow the rain
Will turn to sun
And eventually I will find
The life that I love.

Maybe
At the end of the rainbow
There will be more than a pot of gold,
Maybe
There will be an umbrella left there
For me to hold.

After the Rain

Flowers bloom
Roots run deep
The cost of beauty
Is too often pain.

For brown
To turn green
It needs the sun
But also, the rain.

Often times
We wish success
And then we gripe
When it comes
In the name of strife

But diamonds
Cannot be found
In the open fields,
Instead, it is found
By breaking rocks.

The potter
And the clay,
Mold me, dear one,
Make me useful again.

Dark nights
Of the soul
They come only sometimes
But they never last.

After rain
Comes the sun
And if you're lucky
A rainbow spreads wide

Promises sent
Of better days
Hold your head high
And follow the rain.

Because rain promises
The yellow brick road
To find the pain
But also, the gold.

Love Me or Love Me Not

Love Me
Love Me Not
I pick the petals
One by One.

The flower wilts
The flower fades
Each petal floats
In the wind away.

Love Me
Love Me Not
I am just a girl
Wishing foolishly on petals.

I wish he would
I wish he wouldn't.
He is not the same man
As the one I knew before.

Time travels
Time ticks
If only it could rewind
Before I met him.

64

One look
Changed me forever
Left me here,
Picking petals.

He loves me,
I know indeed.
He loves me not,
He proved that to me.

Spring comes,
Spring fades.
The twist,
The fate.

Leave me here
To pick the petals
Until I fade,
With the flowers I wilted.

Friendship gone,
It withered away.
Too frightened
By the real feelings that came.

Love Me
Love Me Not
A love unrequited,
Will be my song.
Until I die.

About Blair Hayse:

Blair is an International Speaker, Author, and the Founder of Girl on Fire Magazine and Media.

When she is not working the wee hours of the morning with deadlines, she enjoys traveling, shopping, spending time with her children, meeting her best friend for drinks, and pretending like she is not thinking about work while doing all of the above.

Blair loves to read and has written eleven bestselling books including the magic series that has stayed on the bestseller list for four years straight. She is currently working on her first fictional series that she is brave enough to pitch to film based on her own true life story.

Other than that, her life is a series of late nights and lots of coffee.

You can find Blair here:

https://www.facebook.com/writerblairhayse/

https://www.instagram.com/writerblairhayse

https://www.tiktok.com/@writerblairhayse/

www.ingramcontent.com/pod-product-compliance
Lightning Source LLC
LaVergne TN
LVHW041714060526
838201LV00043B/730